I'm Gifting These To You

Keziah Chalkly

Presentation by *BookLeaf Publishing*

Web: www.bookleafpub.com

E-mail: info@bookleafpub.com

ISBN: 9789357440103

First edition 2023

I.

1

Yellow and green leaves
Sing an unknown melody
They leave it behind

I Sold My Thoughts for a Penny

If my thoughts are worth a penny.
What is the price of my secrets…

Do they have any value?

Are you hungry, desperate to cram your greedy
digits into my skull and mush my brain to
sludge, to rummage around and pull out each
thought, like electricity, sending them in through
your fingers and down your spine, ready for
digestion? Dissection. Will you carry them in
your pockets, ready to discard, disregard, litter
the roads with the classified blooms which can
pave the way to my regret. Fashion a bridge over
my soul and into the waves of my heart.

Do you want to hear a secret?

Free of charge,
The penny covers it.

What of the Good Book?

In a hall where a stray cough,
Entices a call and response,
Fragmented beams - slice and melt
Over oak thrones
Reviled and worshiped
With a feast of marble as the dais.

In this chamber of whispers,
Fission will divide the deceit,
Undertoned gasps rip through - bonds.
Obsidian army's scream unvoiced,
On battlefields of aged wood
Soft from the methodical turns of time.

Enclosed with an osculation
Memories of the old ways
Are held in place and bound,
Sewn into the pockets of silence,
A needle through a sob,
A nail through a hand.

In a hall where bones crack against bone
Devotion devoid of understanding,
Stygian stained finger pads,
Pierce through molten air,

Aim engrained in blood,
She bursts into flame.

Doors are Made with Locks

Inhale   ,   exhale.

I got high with my friends, and we laughed. Till our stomachs ached from their spasmodic flailing of the humour which bubbled up from our throats and sored. Popping in the dying breath of dry air. And perhaps about the food we forgot to order, till we were huffed and shoved out of the way by another.

I had a boy in my room that I wanted to kiss. But I left the door unlocked.

I turned my back on him. I cleaned and tidied and sorted away the decaying tranquility of an empty desk. The ghost of hilarity haunting my shoulders, but my lips no longer. As I gave one-word answers that wouldn't tremble as much as my hands.

He stayed on the other side of the room. I don't know if he watched me.

Hot burning, sizzling, searching marked my flesh. Steam rose from my pores. Capturing us in a sphere of warm agitation. Escaping the blistering embrace of imagination. Or was it memory? Goodnight, he left my room, I locked the door.

My body met the floor, as my hands were introduced to my lips, and my cheeks became acquainted with warm salt.

I had wanted to kiss that boy. Before –

Three Years

Three years ago, there was a boy

There was a boy who took her heart with him,
when he left through a door that she didn't want
the key to.

Three years ago, his laughter rang out in her ears
like beautiful tolling bells

And year upon year she chased the sound

Which flowed further away from her desperate
grasp

Clutching only whisps, she stilled in silence.
Waiting for the wind to carry the melody back to
her

But still it danced further away. Lingering on the
glimmering edges of her memory, intangible,
ready to evaporate should she grasp too hard.

And still her heart beat -

Three years ago there was a boy so vibrant, the
sun could do nothing but burn in envy.

The moon tried to soothe its tired rays, passing
over, bringing cool to the ever-growing warmth.

And through that warmth, an anger was born, so
fierce in its blaze that even the sun hid.

But behind that inferno was something else,
something much deeper

Something much darker

It ebbed and flowed, pulsing with her heart,
coursing through her veins

Searing where it touched,

Always present and ever lingering, it lurked in
the chasm

The empty chamber reverberated each echo

And still her heart beat -

She wished for the gift of poetry, and she longed for the release of song. But when he left, he took far more with him

Attentive she would soothe the burns, asleep she would chase his laugh

Haunting her, waking, sometimes she would whisper

Sure no one would hear her muffled cries; she could call out his name

And still her heart beat -

And she cursed it. And she cursed him. Cursed him for leaving her with the poisonous scar of 'why?'

So she cursed the wind and the moon and the sun.

She sentenced the stars and imprisoned the waves.

She banished guilt that seeped through her every pore.

So she stopped. Stilled. Sank.

Deeper she went and her lungs burned, charred
skin screaming

And still her heart beat -

But she refused to surface.

Rain kissed the barrier, loving what had been so
long gone.

Each caress an apology,

For leaving.

And still my heart beat –

II.

In their past wind calls
An old acquaintance forgot
Their eyes don't waver

Twilight Shadows

12

Twilight shadows are dancing across my walls.
The waltzing telephone wires imitate the
intimate –
Rise and fall of a chest,
Leaves turn like the pages of a book they have
yet to become
As branches tap on panes, mocking in morse
code

···· ·_ ···· ·_

I try to erase the hold of his hand on mine
Each swipe, a finger stroke across a keyboard,
an eyelash -
Memories that pool behind my eyelids and step
out single file
Marking their path which tracks like
breadcrumbs.
To forget the boy who can't even remember my
name.

Silent Understanding

My world is one, that moves in the darkness and stills
Very softly, before the flood of lights
Bathe my family. The faces I know.

We breathe in the nirvana of that singular
fractious beat.

Iridescent silk memories lick at the back of my
conscious,
Calling to the realms, ones weakened
Vulnerable to the onslaught,

My family, those who move in the night
Come alive in the light, calling all eyes upon
them.
The most alluring, their attention salutes my
behest.
Promising with my smile,
To those who will never know the truth.

Cold, hard under my feet
I am grounded. I am vapour. I am alive.
Basking in the welcome of cheers,
The sharp warmth that,

Pricks. Marks my nape, as I smile and bow.
Bend.

Always searching for those eyes.

Unspoken Dial Tone

I am sorry you are gone,
Not for yourself but for the man
Who shattered my heart,
When he called me,
As his tears broke through the barrier
Of his tight throat and cracked soul.

I will love him
and
Care for him
and
Treasure him the best way I can-

I'm sorry to you,
That I won't be able to take care of
beautiful son.

I will forget him,
and
I will forget you
and
When he pushes me away-

It will be far in the future
When I think of the boy who cried to me over

the phone.
And my heart will pang,
Because I'll miss him for that second.

Lead and Mercury

Trapped and dragged under. Sharp claws which
rip and tear at skin,
Staining the water maroon. Rosewood tendrils
escape, fleeing and flowing
freely,　　　　　In a way impossible to the
corporeal.　　　Prison. Imprisoned.
Aiming for self-actualization. Achieving the
pinnacle. Succeeding the mandate of humanity
But the hierarchy of needs dictates
that I need　　　　　you
That I am dependent.

Embrace the cacophony of my dichotomy. Wrest
my body,
hold it under, and let the count last longer than
my pulse.
You will not catch the silver whispers which
flow like mercury over your fingers.
Staining and poisoning.
Together we turn
To lead and

Sink.

III.

18

Crystal meets copper
The edge of eternity
Serenity lost

In an Effort to Explain

I write because I've always been told I have a
way with words. And how I can make them
skitter across your teeth fleeting, cold feeling,
mechanical, cog-like, tripping over as undulation
grapples gravity in a grip strong enough to sway
the moon in its orbit and parch the singed,
blood-tinged, dirty grey, and dingy grounds we
call home; but instead are the areas loaned to
each individual, while tears stain faces owned by
people who don't know greed on a first name
basis.

I write because greed is my middle name and I
cling to each word, each phrase, the praise of
being oh so sharp with each remark but cringe
when I rhyme because I never wish to be a slave
to metre or verse or poetics because I'm
"different". I don't write for art.

I write because I get tired of lies which are the
Duracell bunny of my mind, rampant,
demanding attention as I one finger salute the
troops of fears which unhinge the well-oiled
bolts of my breakers, for they are used as often

as I transform oxygen to carbon dioxide. I am a
pollutant and the trees have left me behind.

I write because sometimes the pity and
self-loathing tell me that the stars which burn the
brightest, burn out and I've reached my quota of
gas, alight and alive I have been radiance on a
stake, a sacrificial lamb of a martyr because it's
easier to reduce myself to cinders than let slip
that I am lost in my own galaxy, where the
constellations are wrong and the stars won't lend
me any fuel and I'm running out.

I write because my insides are concrete and
words are wet and thick and tangible, spilling
out means suffocation but I can grab, mould and
wear them, coating delicate with grey, in hopes
that the river will slow as it dries because I can't
keep up. There are too many words and reasons,
there is only so much space in here and eager
violent stampedes crush their way through
barriers, refusing to be bottle-necked, corralled,
coerced into cohesive agreeable families. They
want to be let out and the screaming is butcher
block ready and I can't breathe so

I write

Marks on a Shell

I picked up a shell off the French harbour
seafloor
Winding in amongst the graveyard,
Corpses left-
Tipped and off-kilter
Waiting for the waves to embrace their bodies
And revive them.
I gave that shell to a boy,
A boy with blue eyes who took much more than
that and left behind desolation in the form of
fingerprints.

On that January afternoon,
In clothes that made me feel like a woman
Fingers skimmed the icy,
Sun-dappled mirror,
Breaking,
And picked up a shell from the English harbour
seafloor.
I looked at the boy with brown eyes, who
watched, waiting inches away-
A vessel of warmth.
I put that shell
in my pocket.

Stairs are a Dangerous Thing

I was 9 when I first fell down the stairs.

Grey concrete stairs of my school. My home for the next seven years. I fell and reached the flat part then continued rolling, the momentum of my small body was at a velocity of which I will never know. I was never good a physics. When I reached the bottom I lay there, I thought I was dead. I was sure I was dead. I didn't want to be dead. Everyone gasped and cried out. A man, a father. A father of a friend that was to come in 4 years' time, when my current friends left me because they had too much going on in their lives. A friend that too would leave me when I reached my third set of stairs. She would reach out and cling to the skin of a boy that liked me first. Their breath warm and mixed, in the dark. The father held me in his arms. My small body, too small, too thin, and he said it's OK, it's going to be OK. And the school nurse ran to me, fast, fast, fast. I was important. I don't think I cried. I can't remember crying, because I was dead. But then she wrapped my twisted knee, more for appeasement than necessity, let me rest, and sent me on my way to class. The girl who didn't like

me laughed and said it was because of my hair.
The boy who liked me touched my shoulder,
feather soft and snow gentle like I would shatter
into a million tiny pieces. But I was strong. And
I smiled because his hand was on my shoulder
and I wasn't dead.

I was a teenager when I fell down my second set
of stairs.

Maybe fourteen, fifteen. So ripe in the cruel shift
from innocence to sharp words, like the nails
that now were donned by my friend, who wasn't
my friend anymore, who drew hearts on her
palm because she couldn't feel them any other
way. We used to have twin hearts, tiny, held
together when our fingers interlaced, intertwined
in our own inside jokes. This time it was a carpet
that was my undoing, I would never learn, socks
on the decade-old covering, worn down by the
ceaseless foot traffic of mundane life, erased the
harsh fibres and instead left them with silky
waves, particularly at the crux of each stair. This
time I fell fast, tripped by a phantom playing
games, pushed by the weight of the bitter look
on my friend's, who wasn't my friend anymore,
face when she realized that she was perhaps a
little bit more like her father than she wished to
be. I broke every bone in my body, as my arm

desperately clawed for any purchase on the chipped handrail, which teased just out of reach, I dropped my brand-new laptop. This time I cried, watching as a caricature whimpered right back at me through the black and cracked screen of my new treasure. I closed my eyes, I was convinced I was dead. I wasn't sure if I wanted to be dead. My mother came, fast, fast. Because she heard a noise and needed to investigate. A quick telling off about socks on the stairs and walking with an open laptop, was met with quicker reassurance it would get fixed and the gift of an ice pack for my bruised forearm. The final reflection was of my tear-streaked face, mocking me as shadows danced in the corners of my eyes.

I was 16 when I fell down the stairs again.

Dust had taunted my worn sneaker, made by a child I would never know in a country that I wouldn't visit, all in the name of affordable buying. Marble freckled with a fine covering of particles which had been blown skywards while the land surrounding the brand new, shiny, state-of-the-art school, in the middle of the desert, dredged up an engagement between modern day and historic slavery, so long as it gets built. A time capsule, the minute it was started. I cried out. No one heard. I went to the bathroom, fast. This time I knew I was dead, as I scrambled through the halls which would 'educate' me for the next year. Only moving when the wind would cover the sounds of my steps, ensuring I wouldn't have to meet the faces of those who sang to the shadows which had now found a home in my eyes. In the bathroom, I watched those shadows, the ones who first came to dance on that winter's eve. This time I knew. As the mirror grinned like the Cheshire cat, the shadows left my eyes, soring out above my head and settling down on my shoulders, under my chipped nails, across my stomach and thighs. This, 'breach of uniform' would be my undoing, eventually, I was sure someone would notice and send me straight to the Head. This time I cracked my own smile. Splitting open my face, blood oozed from the idle muscles which had long been in slumber. I wanted to be dead. I screamed it into the face of the girl I barely recognized who sat watching me in every surface. My backpack was the thing that stopped my head from cracking on the granite concrete stairs. In it, the laptop from Christmas, a brand-new pencil case, and books that weighed me down into my own body, holding me captive. I drew a heart on my palm and immediately seared it off with the hottest water, disgusted. I gathered my belongings, my thoughts had long been unattainable, and I left the bathroom, ready to be sent home. No one noticed my uniform, or the terrors which ran up and down the halls with me as I dragged my feet, hoping to see another set of stairs.

Two months later, I caught a boy who fell down the stairs. I caught his small head before it splintered over the corner, where it would ooze warm and gelatinous over my shaking fingers, where I would cry tears into the eyes of a child that I would never know. He looked up at me, embarrassed someone as old as I would bother helping him. I was a god, a saviour, an entity deserving of worship. He blushed and scampered off as his friends jostled him. The liquid did not spill over my fingers, but they did shake. I hoped the boy I would never see again, was sure he was alive. He wanted to be alive.

Call It a Lapse of Judgement

Am I allowed to write you poetry?
Am I allowed to watch as you smile and joke?
The way you tap your foot with your knuckles;
when you hug your shoulders, making your
beautiful body fold away from unwanted
attention.
I know that her gaze is the one you want to be
meeting, but as you lock with my innocent eyes,
I can't help that my heart sways.

So, I hide it away.
Chains that make my muscles scream, heaving
their biting weight
Vicious, rusted, splitting, splintering my skin
Metal serpentine
Winds, intertwining, around appendages that
have no fight left to give.
Banished, abused.
The sweet harmless enemy
Is left bruised and bleeding and punished.

For noticing how you tuck your thumbs into
your jumper to stop them nervously fidgeting.

Am I allowed to write you poetry?

Am I allowed to wonder how your face changes
when you see her?
Knowing that it's not me you see when you
look, when you tuck that escaped mahogany,
not golden,
tendril back into the knot which held it.

Knowing it will be the only knot tied between
us,
I secure it tighter.

Keys to the lock,
Hang around my neck,
The weight breaks my gaze finally

This is the first, last and -
only.

IV.

A lone figure waits
Redemption now turns away
Sand falls through once more

fairytaletiming

Now's not the time to say I love you. Because
we're both just so busy, and I want it to mean

something

When that first circular-shaped word, jams open
your mouth, ready for the surge of that guerrilla
style, privately trained, secret black ops,
top-notch onslaught……
No no, now is simply not the time to say I love
you.
Because you're running late and I've already
missed the last train, I watched seconds tick by,
march on, salute, regroup and meander away…
and now I've missed the train and don't take that
tone with me because the last train is gone but
you don't know that

I am

it

Now's really not the time to say I love you
because I've not had a chance to hang out my
laundry – it's unwashed. I've not aired it and

look please hear me when I say it's not the time, because you haven't even seen my blue shirt or the green military uniform in its most pressed, impressive, state, you've not seen my moth-bitten cardigan, gosh they're always so hungry. But you haven't seen it so now's not the time, no really it isn't, no, wait-

Now isn't the time to say I love you. Because this time, this time, I might listen, I might say it back. No, but, I've got my music GCSE to study for and yes I know I'm 21, and yes I know I already took that exam 6 years ago but what if it runs out? Like, expires, what if the music has changed and I need to renew it? Before it was focused on Mozart's Symphony No. 11 in D Major, but now I think it's a call and response with Siegfried Sassoon as the lyricist. It's tricky these days trying to stay on top of the times, the trends, things. Desirable – I mean dedicated. Yes dedicated to getting a piece of paper that says wow look how clever you are, and then I can pop it up on the fridge and show you.

Hello, it's been a while. I can see you're busy, but I just wanted to let you know I've bought the train tickets. And the laundry is washed and put away. And if you - if you just – look – please look-

No please come back –
-look at the fridge.
But it's all done. It's all done now and I have
something to tell you

I –

Yes. Yes, you really should be getting on.
Goodbye.

Dear Mr. John Green

Dear Mr. John Green,

Would you like to write a story about me? One that will get turned into a film. A film that I can be the main character in?

Not a Looking for Alaska or a Fault in Our Stars, where I go through the most life-altering, soul-ripping trauma 'balanced' out by one fleeting moment for overdramatized happiness. I don't want my face to have a wistful smile, thinking back with gratitude about getting to know someone for a millisecond before the screen clicks to black and the credits begin to roll. Poetically, it's beautiful, but not for my story. I'm thinking more of a… a…, are there any truly happy endings? Where no one dies, or leaves, or maybe. Where they are able to overcome everything with the power of love.

It can be a tearjerker, but not too sad because my grandmother doesn't like films that make her sad. I don't think my mother does either. Don't make my family sad when you write a story about me. A story that will be made into a film.

A film that I can be the star of, right Mr. Green?

34

Mr. Green?

I would really like it if you could give it a happy ending. But you seem to struggle with those as much as I do…

Beautiful, and

The words on the pages are the ones that have
always been,
carved into the skin of those waiting,
waging a war, that has gone on for centuries.
A name.
For each one, celebrating their creation.
Naming them as nothing more,
A title
A label
A statement
A name allocating their station.
Words which mock
Which blame which strangle and suffocate.
Never able to hold a candle to its worn with
pain.
Unrelenting.
Raining down whispers which break the skin.
The arrow can never miss, the bullseye written
with curving swooping letters calling:
Beautiful.

Tulips in 2022

There were tulips on a bench in 2022,
And the sliver credit card of a plaque,
Giving a name and
When they arrived and left this plane,
Numerals of life's transactions.
Read,
in memoriam.
I don't remember the name,
It will never be one that I care about
But I will remember the tulips in
2022
When the timestamped digits
Remind me they couldn't have lasted since
2004.
When my breath rips from my lungs,
And hides in my throat,
Bashful to be surging in defiance
Faced with such grief-stricken love,
Which stands the test of time,
18 years between.
A demonstration to a young woman in
2022
That this name who I will never
Care about, will be
Remembered.
Will those tulips ever be mine?

Ode to Home

Tell me.
What am I expected to do when my cultural
identity does not align with my ethnicity,
and how do I face the socio-normative
aggravations that call out 'cultural appropriation'
when I am simply to trying share with them the
beautiful wash of customs that I have been
bathed in since they were raised in a world so
different from the one that I know.

Tell me.
How do I go back? To the places that knew,
which understood, they were a home in a long
queue
of homes to come. A place that welcomed
anyone and everyone, and wrapped a scarf
around your
neck before you headed out on your next
adventure, the packed lunch of diversity it had
gifted you, warming your hands and your heart.

Tell me.
Why you refuse to take a moment before you
hurl around accusations because these 'things'
don't come from your 'nations'.

Because they come from mine.
All of them.

Every country, every culture, every person has
become an amalgamation that some will never
try to understand.
Of whom I am and who I always will be because
those homes gave me so much more than just a
house.
And you would be blessed to know the
difference between a sari and a shalwar kameez,
to know the steps to the dances at Jāṇi, and to
know the words to the Egyptian national anthem
and be able to sing them with pride. These gifts
and treasures are things you tell me I need to
hide because they don't reflect what you see.

Tell me.
Why is it that when you look at me you can't see
who I see when I gaze into the mirror of my life?
So, please. Close your eyes and let me take you
around the world.
Let me show you my home.